Book 2

Your First Keyboard Method

Mary Thompson

Chester Music

(A division of Music Sales Limited)

8/9 Frith Street, London W1V 5TZ

About Book 2

Following on from Book 1 in the series, this book will help you to develop your keyboard skills one step at a time. In Book 1 you learned the names of the white notes, and some of the signs and symbols used in music. In Book 2 you will learn about the black keys, and you will begin to play tunes with both hands at the same time.

Here are some reminders of the things you learned in Book 1. See how many you can remember.

This is a semibreve, or whole note. It lasts for four beats.

This is a minim, or half note. It lasts for two beats.

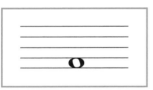

This is a crotchet, or quarter note. It lasts for one beat.

This is a time signature.

$$\frac{3}{4}$$

This is a treble clef.

This is a bass clef.

This is a repeat sign.

***P* is short for *piano*. It means "play quietly".**

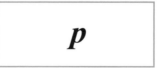

p

This book © Copyright 1998 Chester Music.
Order No. CH61408   ISBN 0-7119-6789-X

Music and text setting by Mary Thompson
Illustrations by Nigel Hooper
Cover design by Ian Butterworth
Printed in the United Kingdom by Printwise (Haverhill) Limited, Haverhill, Suffolk.

Notes you have learned so far

Here you can see all the notes you learned in Book 1.

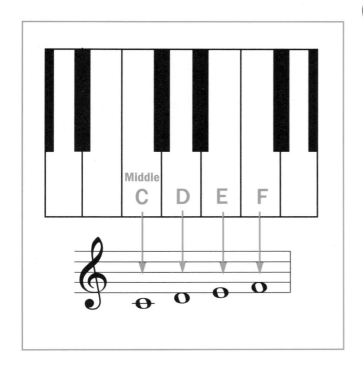

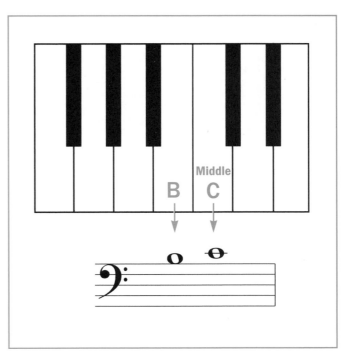

These are the notes you learned to play with your right hand.

These are the notes you learned to play with your left hand.

Playing loudly

In Book 1 you learned the Italian word *piano*, which means "quietly". Sometimes you have to play the music loudly. The Italian word for "loudly" is *forte*. The word *forte* is often shortened to *f*.

If you are learning on a piano, press the keys harder to play loudly. If you are learning on an electronic keyboard, you can adjust the volume control so the sound is louder.

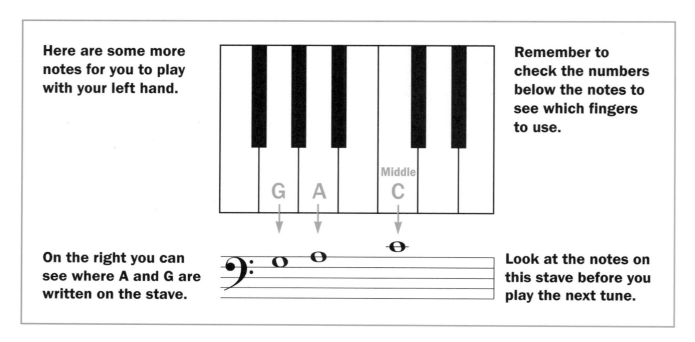

Here are some more notes for you to play with your left hand.

Remember to check the numbers below the notes to see which fingers to use.

On the right you can see where A and G are written on the stave.

Look at the notes on this stave before you play the next tune.

Left A Bit

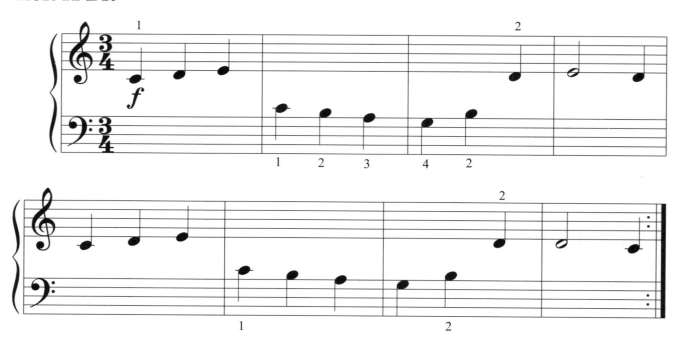

The picture on the right shows you where to find G for your right hand.

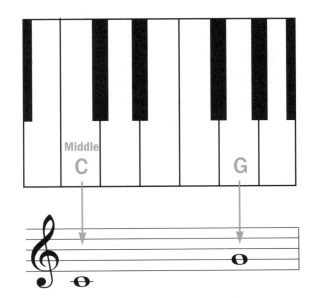

Remember, a number 5 over a note tells you to use your little finger.

Here you can see where G is written on the stave.

See if you can spot G in the tune below.

Marching On

Remember to play the tune on this page loudly.

Dotted notes

Sometimes there is a dot after a note. This makes the note last for one and a half times its normal length. For example, a minim lasts for two beats, so a minim with a dot after it lasts for three beats. When there is a dot after a note, it is called a dotted note.

This is a dotted minim. Dotted minims are also called dotted half notes.

Dot To Dot

Remember to play this tune quietly.

Leaving gaps in music

There are signs in music that tell you to leave gaps. These gaps are called rests. When you see a rest, count the correct number of beats in your head, before playing the next note.

A semibreve rest is also used to show a rest which lasts for a whole bar.

A crotchet (or quarter) rest = 1 beat

A minim (or half) rest = 2 beats

A semibreve (or whole) rest = 4 beats

Missing Beats

All the gaps in this tune have been filled with rests. Count very carefully and remember to lift your fingers off the keys when you see a rest.

You can practise counting this rhythm by clapping the beats. Miss one clap for a crotchet rest and two claps for a minim rest.

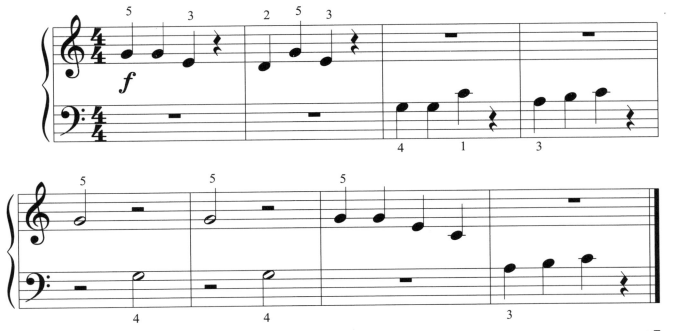

Playing two notes at the same time

So far you have only played one note at a
time. Now you will start playing two notes
together. Don't worry if you find it a bit
difficult at first. The more you practise,
the easier it will become. There are some
tips below to help you.

*Read the tips below
before you try
"Double Trouble".*

Double Trouble

Practice hints

- Practise with each hand on its
  own at first, until you can play
  both parts without any mistakes.

- When you are sure of the notes,
  try playing the tune with both
  hands together.

- Remember to use the correct
  fingers for each note.

- Start off very slowly, then
  gradually play the music faster
  until you are playing at a
  comfortable speed.

8

Another note-length

Here you are going to learn about a shorter note, called a quaver. A quaver lasts for half a crotchet beat. It looks like a crotchet with a tail.

Quavers are often joined together in groups of two or four. This makes them easier to read. You can see what they look like below.

These are quavers. Quavers are also called eighth notes.

| This is how two quavers are joined together. | |

| This is how four quavers are joined together. | |

Daybreak

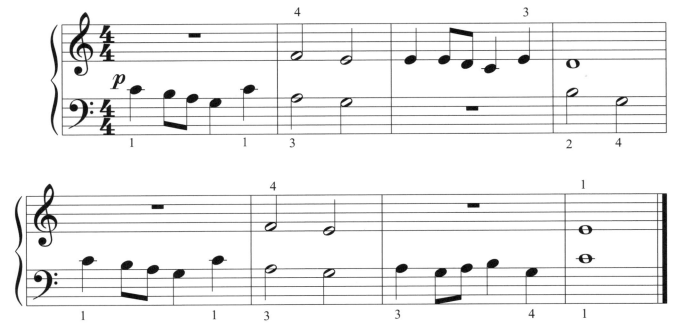

Using the black keys

Sometimes the black keys are called sharp notes, and sometimes they are called flat notes. A sign in front of a note tells you whether it is sharp or flat. A sharp sign in front of a note tells you to press the next key to the right of that note.

This is what a sharp sign looks like. When a note is sharp, it sounds slightly higher.

On the right you can see where to find F sharp on your keyboard.

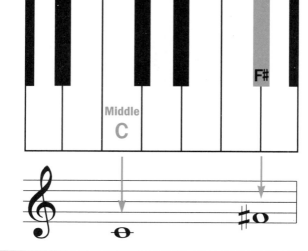

When an F has a sharp sign in front of it, any Fs after it in that bar are also F sharps.

Here you can see how F sharp is written on the stave.

Play F, then F sharp. Can you hear the difference?

Look Sharp!

10

A flat sign in front of a note tells you to press the next key to the left of that note. When a note is flat, it sounds slightly lower. On the left you can see what a flat sign looks like. Watch out for the flat signs in "Feeling Flat Blues".

On the right you can see where to find B flat on your keyboard.

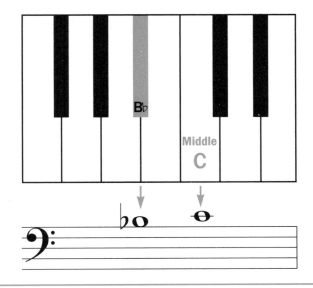

When a B has a flat sign in front of it, any Bs after it in that bar are also B flat.

Here you can see how B flat is written on the stave.

Play B, then B flat. Can you hear the difference?

Feeling Flat Blues

Dotted crotchets

A dotted crotchet lasts for one and a half crotchet beats. You can see what a dotted crotchet looks like on the right. To play dotted crotchets, it helps to count "one and two and". Before you play the next tune, try clapping the rhythm.

This is a dotted crotchet. Dotted crotchets are also called dotted half notes.

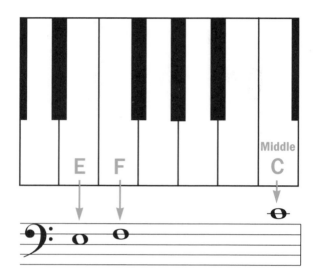

On the right you can see where to find E and F for your left hand.

Remember to check the numbers below the notes to see which fingers to use.

Here you can see where E and F are written on the stave.

Look at the notes on this stave before you start to play.

Summer Song

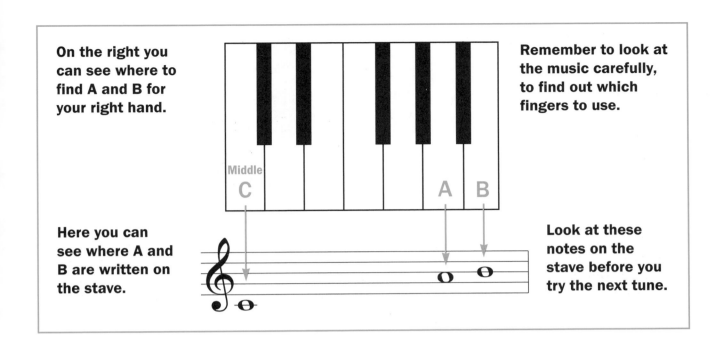

On the right you can see where to find A and B for your right hand.

Remember to look at the music carefully, to find out which fingers to use.

Here you can see where A and B are written on the stave.

Look at these notes on the stave before you try the next tune.

Twinkle, Twinkle, Little Star

Playing smoothly

The Italian word *legato* tells you to play the music smoothly. Sometimes a curved line, called a slur, tells you to play *legato*. To play smoothly, press a key and, as you are lifting your finger, begin to press down the next key.

Play the tune below as smoothly as you can.

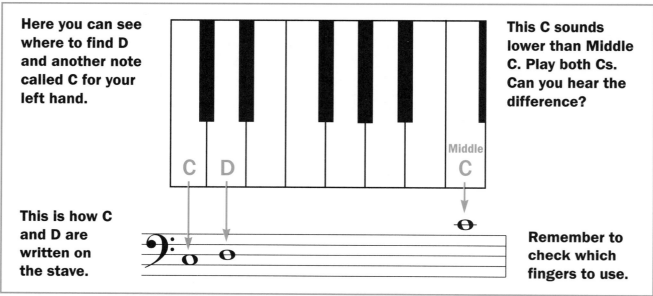

Here you can see where to find D and another note called C for your left hand.

This C sounds lower than Middle C. Play both Cs. Can you hear the difference?

This is how C and D are written on the stave.

Remember to check which fingers to use.

Frère Jacques

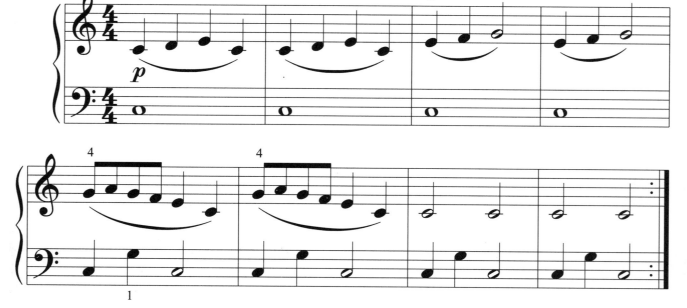

Another Italian word

The Italian word *staccato* means "short and detached". A dot above or below a note tells you to play *staccato*. To play notes *staccato*, strike the key, then remove your finger as quickly as possible. Try to play *staccato* notes as short as you can.

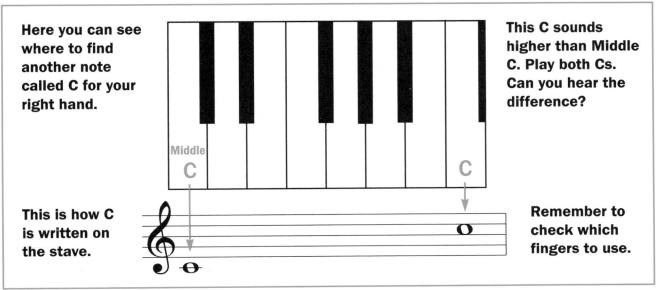

Here you can see where to find another note called C for your right hand.

This C sounds higher than Middle C. Play both Cs. Can you hear the difference?

This is how C is written on the stave.

Remember to check which fingers to use.

The Porcupine's Picnic

Congratulations!

Now that you have reached the end of the book, here is a special piece for you play. Practise it until you can play it all the way through without any mistakes. Then you can play it to a friend or relative, to show them what you have learned.

Party Time

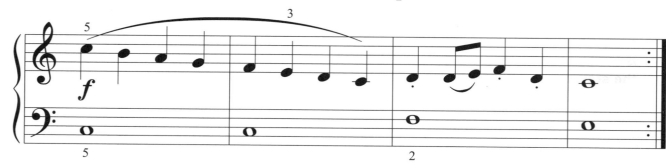